Table of Contents

I0170524

Amazing Restaurant Meals You Can Trust

Unique Must-try restaurant Recipes

BY: Ida Smith

Copyright © 2020 by Ida Smith. All Rights Reserved.

License Notes

This book is licensed for your personal enjoyment only. This book may not be re-sold or given away to other people. If you would like to share this book with another person, please purchase an additional copy for each recipient. If you're reading this book and did not purchase it, or it was not purchased for your use only, then please return to your favorite ebook retailer and purchase your own copy. Thank you for respecting the hard work of this author.

Introduction

In recent times, the world economy has declined greatly and people are no longer spending money lavishly. Cutting down on so many expenses and living by the budget has become the order of the day; hence, people find it difficult to visit their favorite restaurants to have that special meal they love. Are you one of those craving your favorite restaurant meal? This cookbook has some amazing restaurant meals that you must try, and instead of sulking because you can't visit the restaurant, step into your kitchen and turn your home into the restaurant by preparing the meal you crave.

Cheesy macaroni

Macaroni mixed with cheese has always been some people's favorite meal and most families order this from their favorite restaurant. However, with this recipe, you can make it from the comfort of your kitchen.

Cooking Time: 40 minutes
Yield: 5
List of Ingredients:

- 6 ounces of pasta
- 1/2 cup of butter
- 1 small minced onion
- 1/3 cup of flour
- 3 cups of milk
- 1 cup of cheese

- 1/2 tablespoon of salt
- 1/3 teaspoon of ground black pepper
- 1/3 teaspoon of mustard powder

Preparation:

Preheat your oven to about 360°. Boil your pasta following the instructions on the pack. Drain out the water and set aside.

Melt your butter in a pan, add your onion and flour and let it simmer for about 5 minutes or until it is thick. Add your milk and cook, then add your cheese, salt, pepper, and mustard, cook until the cheese melts. Add your pasta and pour the mixture into a casserole dish and bake for 30 minutes, remove and serve.

Chicken and lime

This is one meal you are sure to enjoy with your family, and you can have this as a nice breakfast.

Cooking Time: 2 hours 20 minutes

Yield: 4

List of Ingredients:

- 1/3 cup of lime juice
- 1/3 cup of tequila
- 1 pound of chicken breast, skinless and boneless
- 3 tablespoons of dressing
- 1 tablespoon of salsa
- 1/3 cup of tortilla chips
- 1/3 cup of shredded cheddar cheese

Preparation:

Pour your tequila and lime juice into a plastic bag and seal it. Add your chicken and let it sit for 2 hours. Heat up your grill and your broiler, remove the chicken from the liquids, and grill for about 10 minutes.

Mix your salsa and dressing in a bowl and set aside. Scatter your chips in your oven plate, place your chicken on the chips, pour your dressing mix on it, place your cheese on it, place your oven plate in a broiler, and heat until the cheese melts and serve hot.

Mixed beans salad

You must be used to the normal salad you make at home, however, the beans salad is one that you must try, it comes with a unique taste.

Cooking Time: 20 minutes

Yield: 4

List of Ingredients:

- 1 can of green beans
- 1 can of kidney beans
- 1 can of wax beans
- 1 medium-sized green pepper, diced
- 1 medium-sized white onion, diced
- 1 cup of oil
- 1/3 cup of vinegar

- 3 tablespoons of sugar
- 1 tablespoon of salt
- 1 teaspoon of black pepper

Preparation:

Drain all the beans and mix them in a bowl and mix your salt, pepper, onions, vinegar, sugar, and oil stir properly and cover, chill till you are ready to serve.

Fried mushrooms and steak

Steaks are great, and having it with your fried mushroom is the best thing that can happen to you. Don't bother going to the restaurant, just prepare it by yourself.

Cooking Time: 30 minutes

Yield: 4

List of Ingredients:

- – 1 cup of beef broth
- – 1 medium-sized onions, diced
- – 2 cups of mushrooms and the juice
- – 1/3 cup of burgundy wine

Preparation:

Place your beef broth in a pan, add your onions and let it simmer for about 15 minutes. Ass your mushroom and wine and cook for another 15 minutes and serve.

Hard rock coleslaw

If you want something light but delicious, then this meal is the perfect dish for you.

Cooking Time: 20 minutes

Yield: 4

List of Ingredients:

- − 1/2 cup of mayonnaise
- − 2 tablespoons of white vinegar
- − 1/2 cup of granulated sugar
- − 1/3 cup of milk
- − 1/2 teaspoon of salt
- − 1 head of chopped cabbage
- − 1 cup of shredded carrot

Preparation:

Mix your mayonnaise, vinegar, milk, sugar, and salt together in a bowl until it becomes very smooth. Add your cabbage and carrot into the mixture and mix well. Cover it and chill before serving.

Chicken in orange sauce

This is the kind of meal people go to have in the restaurant but it is something you can put together within a few minutes from the comfort of your kitchen.

Cooking Time: 20 minutes
Yield: 4
List of Ingredients:

- 1 pack of frozen chicken
- 1 medium-sized onion, well chopped
- 1 bell of green pepper, well diced
- 1 cup of oil
- 2 cups of orange sauce
- 2 cups of cooked rice

Preparation:

Preheat your oven to about 300°. Place your chicken in the oven and let it bake for about 20 minutes or until it is tender. Remove from oven and set aside.

Heat up your oil in a pan, add your onions and pepper into the pan and let it simmer for 5 minutes, then add your orange sauce and allow it to cook a while.

Add your chicken into the pan and stir until the chicken is well coated in your sauce, then serve it with your rice.

Meatballs in areas crumbs

Forget about craving for the restaurant kind of meatballs and make this specialty in your home for your loved ones and enjoy.

Cooking Time: 40 minutes
Yield: 6
List of Ingredients:

- 1 pound of beef, ground
- 1/3 pound of pork, ground
- 1/3 cup of breadcrumbs
- 4 cloves of minced garlic
- 2 big eggs
- 2 green onions, minced
- 1 small-sized yellow onions, minced

- 3 tablespoons of parmesan cheese
- 1 tablespoon of grated romano cheese
- 3 tablespoons of fresh parsley, minced
- 2 tablespoons of minced basil
- 1 teaspoon of salt
- 1/2 teaspoon of pepper
- 1 cup of oil

Preparation:

Heat up your oven to about 360°. Mix all your ingredients in a bowl except the oil, roll the mixture in a bowl, and set aside.

Heat your oil in a pan, place your meatballs in the oil, put in your oven, and bake for about 30 minutes until it turns brown. Remove from oven and the oil and drain in your paper towel.

Chicken wrapped in lettuce

This is a great and tasty meal that most people are craving for. Wrapping your chicken with lettuce makes it more fun and tasty to cook and eat.

Cooking Time: 40 minutes
Yield: 6
List of Ingredients:

- 2 lb. of chicken breast, boneless
- 1 teaspoon of fresh ground black pepper
- 1/2 cup of oil
- 1 bunch of chopped green onions
- 1 cup of chopped water chestnuts
- 2 cloves of well-minced garlic
- 1 cup of soy sauce
- 1/3 cup of vinegar
- 1/2 teaspoon of cayenne pepper

- 1 teaspoon of sugar
- 2 tablespoons of cornstarch
- 1 cup of lettuce, iceberg

Preparation:

Chop your chicken breast into small bits, sprinkle your black pepper and a little soy sauce on it. Heat up your oil in a pan and fry your chicken.

When the chicken is well cooked, add your garlic to the chicken in the pan, add your green onions and water chestnuts and let it cook for about 5 minutes. Then, add your vinegar, soy sauce, cornstarch, sugar, and cayenne pepper, stir properly and allow it to cook until it begins to bubble.

Remove from heat, spread your lettuce on a plate, and serve your chicken mix wrapped in the lettuce.

Mussel and pasta

Having a nice seafood with pasta is the best way to start the day, it is spicy and delicious.

Cooking Time: 20 minutes

Serve: 4

List of Ingredients:

- 3 big shrimp
- 3 scallops
- 6 big mussels
- 1 cup of marinara sauce
- 1/2 teaspoon of salt
- 1/2 teaspoon of white pepper
- 12 ounce of pasta

Preparation:

Cook your shrimps, mussels, scallop, sauce, salt, and pepper for about 5 minutes, until your shrimp turns pink and your mussels open.

Toss your pasta into the pan, mix properly, cover for about 5 minutes and serve.

Tilapia In garlic and lime

Tilapia isn't just a very nutritious meal, it is also very tasty. However, combining it with your garlic makes it yummier. And this dish is also perfect for your family.

Cooking Time: 20 minutes
Yield: 4
List of Ingredients:

- 3 tablespoons of butter
- 2 cloves of crushed garlic
- 4 ounces of tilapia fillet
- 1 teaspoon of bay seasoning
- 1/3 cup of lime juice

Preparation:

Melt your butter in a large pan, add your garlic and simmer for 2 minutes.

Season your fish with your bay seasoning on both sides and place it in your pan. Allow it to cook until it becomes golden brown then you flip the other, cook for a few minutes, then add your lime juice into the pan, cover it, and let it cook for few more minutes.

Remove from pan and serve with anything of your choice.

Buttered fried rice and eggs

Let's prepare this special bowl of buttered fried rice and enjoy it with your family.

Cooking Time: 20 minutes
Yield: 4
List of Ingredients:

- 1/2 cup of butter
- 1 medium-sized of onions, diced
- 1 cup of well-chopped carrot
- 2 cups of chopped green onions
- 2 tablespoons of sesame seeds
- 5 big eggs
- 1 cup of boiled rice
- 1/2 tablespoon of soy sauce

– 1/2 teaspoon of salt

– 1/2 teaspoon of pepper

Preparation:

Melt your butter in a pan, add your onions, carrots, and green onions fry for 5 minutes, and set aside. Preheat your oven to about 300°. Place your sesame seeds in a pan and bake for 15 minutes. Grease another pan and pour your eggs inside, scramble it.

Mix your rice, sesame seeds, soy sauce, vegetables, salt, and pepper, and serve.

Tomato salad and spaghetti

When you serve your family with this meal, they will be quite impressed and feel like they are in their favorite restaurant.

Cooking Time: 30 minutes
Yield: 4
List of Ingredients:

- 1 pack of spaghetti
- ½ cup of oil
- 6 cloves of well-chopped garlic
- 8 fillet of anchovy
- 1 tablespoon of red pepper flakes, crushed
- 1 cup of fresh parsley leaf

Preparation:

Boil your spaghetti according to the instructions on the pack. Drain and set aside. Heat your oil in a pan, add the garlic and cook for 1 minute. Add your anchovies and let them cook while you break them with your spoon.

Add your pepper flakes, and toss in your drained spaghetti and stir properly. Add your parsley, stir well, and serve hot.

Pasta and chicken with chili

A bowl of spicy pasta is great for your family at dinner. Let's try it!

Cooking Time: 20 minutes

Yield: 4

List of Ingredients:

- 2 pounds of chicken breast, boneless and skinless
- 1 tablespoon of cajun seasoning
- 2 tablespoons of butter
- 1 cup of heavy cream
- 1/3 teaspoon of basil
- 1/2 teaspoon of lemon pepper seasoning
- 1/2 teaspoon of salt
- 1 teaspoon of pepper

- 1 teaspoon of garlic powder
- 4oz of cooked linguine
- 1 teaspoon of grated parmesan

Preparation:

Place your chicken and your seasoning in a bag, seal, and shake well to coat. Melt your butter in a pan, place your chicken in the pan, and simmer for 5 minutes. Add your heavy cream, lemon seasoning, and stir until the sauce thickens, add your pasta mix properly.

Add your parmesan and serve.

Baked potato and steak

Baking your sweet potatoes tastes better than frying it, and this is one meal that most people order from the restaurant.

Cooking Time:70 minutes
Yield: 4
List of Ingredients:

- 4 big sweet potatoes
- ½ cup of oil
- 3 tablespoons of sugar
- 1 tablespoon of ground cinnamon
- 1/2 cup of butter

Preparation:

Heat up the oven to about 300 degrees. Brush a little oil on the skin of your potatoes and bake for about 60 minutes. When it is well baked and the outside is dark, just know that it will be done inside.

While your potato is baking, mix your sugar and cinnamon in a bowl. Bring out your potato, divide into two, add your butter and sprinkle your cinnamon mixture on it and serve.

Vegetable pizza

This recipe is for all the pizza lovers out there! Let's prepare this delicious pizza at home and have a full day with your family.

Cooking Time: 25 minutes
Yield: 6
List of Ingredients:

- – 1 cup of flour
- – 1/2 cup of artichoke dip
- – 1/2 teaspoon of seasoning
- – 1/2 teaspoon of black pepper
- – 1 teaspoon of salt
- – 1/2 cup of mushroom, sliced
- – 1/2 cup of tomatoes, diced

- 1 teaspoon of garlic powder
- 1/3 cup of shredded cheese
- 1 tablespoon of parmesan

Preparation:

Heat up your oven to 360°. Spray cooking spray on your pizza pan, place your flour in the pan. Mix your dip and other spices in a bowl, spread the mixture over your flour, top it with your tomatoes, cheese, and mushrooms, bake for about 15 minutes and serve.

Pancakes made from pumpkins

As the holiday approaches, treat your family with these amazing pancakes.

Cooking Time: 30 minutes

Yield: 8

List of Ingredients:

- 2 big eggs
- 2 cups of buttermilk
- 4 tablespoons of melted butter
- 1/2 can of pumpkin
- 2 tablespoons of sugar
- 1/3 teaspoon of salt
- 2 cups of flour
- 1/2 teaspoon of baking powder

- 1/3 teaspoon of baking soda
- 1/2 teaspoon of ground cinnamon
- 1/3 teaspoon of allspice
- 1 tablespoon of oil

Preparation:

Heat up your skillet and coat your pan with a little oil. Mix your eggs in a large bowl, add your buttermilk, salt, sugar, pumpkin, and butter in a bowl and blend well with a blender. In another bowl, mix your flour, baking powder, baking soda, sugar, cinnamon, allspice, and salt.

Slowly add your egg mixture into the flour mixture and mix properly until your batter is well mixed. Carefully place your batter in batches into your pan, simmer for about 5 minutes, flip the other side and let it cook until it becomes brown, remove and serve warm.

Sweet potato in honey

Sweet potato and Honey is a meal that is commonly found in some traditional restaurants and it tastes great.

Cooking Time: 60 minutes
Yield: 1
List of Ingredients:

- – 1 big potato
- – 2 tablespoons of shortening
- – 2 tablespoons of salt
- – 2 tablespoons of butter
- – 2 tablespoons of honey
- – 1/2 tablespoon of cinnamon

Preparation:

Preheat your oven to about 300°. Brush your potato with your shortening and sprinkle salt on it. Put in your oven and bake for 50 minutes until it is tender.

Divide your potatoes into 2, whisk your butter and honey together, out on each side of your potato, sprinkle your cinnamon on it and serve.

Rice in almond flavor

This is a simple and unique dish that can go with chicken that you are grilling for your family.

Cooking Time: 40 minutes

Yield: 6

List of Ingredients:

- 1/3 cup of butter
- 1 cup of rice
- 3 cups of chicken broth
- 1/2 teaspoon of salt
- 1/3 cup of silver almonds
- 1/2 cup.of celery, diced
- 1/3 cup of onions, diced
- 1 tablespoon of dried parsley

Preparation:

Melt your butter in a pan and add your rice into your pan and let it simmer for about 5 minutes or until it turns light brown. While your rice is on fire, microwave your chicken broth and add it to the pan, add your salt, cover and let it boil for about 20 minutes.

Melt your remaining butter in another pan, add your almonds and simmer for 2 minutes. Add your celery and onions and fry for another 2 minutes.

When your rice is properly cooked, remove it from heat, then add your almond mix to the rice and your parsley cover it for 5 minutes and serve hot.

Shredded lettuce and fish tacos

You can have this delicious meal of grilled fish with your family at any time of the day, such as breakfast, lunch, or even dinner.

Cooking Time: 5 minutes
Yield: 1
List of Ingredients:

- 1 tortilla flour
- 1 battered fish fillet
- 1/3 cup of shredded lettuce

Preparation:

Heat your tortilla flour in a microwave for about 1 minute to get soft. Place your fish filler in the middle of the tortilla, add your lettuce to the fish, fold and serve.

Pork sausage and eggs

Now, you can prepare the restaurant kind of breakfast that you have been craving by following this unique recipe.

Cooking Time: 30 minutes
Yield: 4
List of Ingredients:

- 4 oz of pork sausage
- 2 medium-sized onions, diced
- 4 big eggs, whisked
- 1 teaspoon of green chilies, minced
- 1 teaspoon of salt
- 1/2 teaspoon of pepper
- 4 cups of flour

– 4 slices of cheese

Preparation:

Heat up your pan and add your onions and sausage into the pan and let it simmer for 5 minutes or until the sausage is brown. Add your chilies, fry for another minute, then pour your whisked eggs into the pan and combine with the sausage mixture. Season it with your salt and pepper.

Place your cheese into the microwave and heat up. Add your egg mixture and cheese together and serve.

Double beef burger

Another way to prepare your favorite burger with beef and some salad dressing.

Cooking Time: 30 minutes

Yield: 2

List of Ingredients:

- 2 plain hamburger bun
- 1 pound of ground beef
- 4 slices of cheese
- 1 tablespoon of salad dressing
- 1 bell of fresh tomato, sliced
- 2 lettuce leaves
- 1 small onion, sliced

Preparation:

Preheat your grill and divide each hamburger bun into tap and toast lightly and set aside. Divide your beef into portions, season it with salt and pepper and let it cook for 5 minutes. Place one slice of cheese on each burger bun, and melt the cheese.

Place your salad dressing, tomato, lettuce, onion, and beef on the bun, cover with the other bun and serve.

Cheese sandwich and eggs

This kind of sandwich is always served in restaurants like McDonald's, but with these recipes, you can make it from your own kitchen.

Cooking Time: 15 minutes

Yield: 4

List of Ingredients:

- 1 beefsteak halved
- 2 teaspoons of Worcestershire sauce
- 1 teaspoon of garlic salt
- 1 small-sized onions, minced
- 3 tablespoons of butter
- 2 bagels, split
- 2 medium-sized eggs

– 2 slices of cheese

Preparation:

Place your steak and Worcestershire sauce in a plastic bag, add your garlic salt and onions in it, and grill for 5 minutes, remove and set aside. Butter your bagels inside and grill.

Whisk your eggs in a bowl, heat a little oil in a pan, and fry your eggs. Once it is dried, fold it into two and cut it into four. Place your steak at the bottom of your bagel, place your eggs on it, add your cheese and top with the other side of your bagel and serve.

Cheeseburger and bacon

This cheeseburger is a fast food meal that you can have with your family, and this can be made from the comfort of your home.

Cooking Time: 10 minutes
Yield: 2
List of Ingredients:

- 2 onions ring, frozen
- 1/2 pound of ground beef
- 2 slices of bacon
- 2 hamburger bun
- 1 sesame seed
- 3 tablespoons of barbeque sauce
- 1 slice of cheese

Preparation:

Using the directions on the pack of your onions, bake it. Cook your hamburger for about 5 minutes on both sides. In a small pan, fry your bacon until it becomes crispy, spread your barbeque sauce on one side of your hamburger.

Place your onion ring, cheese, and bacon on it, cover with the other side and serve.

Cheese fries in Texas style

Do you crave that Texas style of cheese fries, no need to worry; here is the perfect recipe for you.

Cooking Time: 40 minutes

Yield: 4

List of Ingredients:

- 1 bag of steak fries
- 4 slices of bacon
- 1 jalapeno pepper, sliced
- 1 pack of cheddar cheese, shredded

Preparation:

Spread your fries on a cookie sheet, put them in your oven, and bake following the instructions on the pack. Line your bacon on another sheet, and bake for about 20 minutes or until it is crispy. When both fries and bacon are done, remove them from the oven.

Add your cheese and jalapeno to the fries, scatter your bacon on it, bake for another 10 minutes or until your cheese melts, remove from oven and serve while sizzling.

Deep chicken fries

This is an easy to make restaurant recipe and it can serve your family a nice breakfast.

Cooking Time: 30 minutes

Yield: 5

List of Ingredients:

- 1 pack of chicken breast, boneless and skinless
- 1/3 cup of flour
- 1/2 cup of fish fry
- 1 big egg
- 1/3 cup of water
- 1 cup of oil

Preparation:

Cut your chicken breasts in bits like your French fries, put your Flour and fish fry in a plastic bag, cover, and set aside. Whisk your egg in a bowl with a little water.

Dip your chicken into the flour bag, dip in your egg mix, shake off the excess, and keep aside. Heat your oil in a pan and fry your chicken until it becomes brown, drain on a paper towel, and serve.

Steak deep-fried rolls

Looking for an amazing appetizer? This Chinese meal is your go-to choice for an appetizer.

Cooking Time: 20 minutes

Yield: 4

List of Ingredients:

- 2 cups of oil
- 2 medium-sized onions, diced
- 7 slices of steak
- 1/2 teaspoon of salt
- 1/2 teaspoon of pepper
- 5oz of cheez wiz
- 10 wraps of egg roll

Preparation:

Heat a little oil in a pan, add your onion and let it cook for 3 minutes, break your steak and add it to the skillet, sprinkle your salt and pepper and cook for another 10 minutes. Remove from heat and set aside.

Place your egg roll wrap on a surface, place your beef and onions on it, wrap it, and top it with your cheez wiz. Fold the sides and seal with water.

Heat your oil in a pan and carefully add your rolls and deep fry until it turns golden brown, remove from oil, drain with your paper towel and serve.

Pretzels and butter

This is a popular meal that everyone loves. But now, you can make this simple meal from the comfort of your home.

Cooking Time: 60 minutes
Yield: 4
List of Ingredients:

- 2 cups of warm water
- 2 tablespoons of sugar
- 1/2 cup of yeast
- 1 tablespoon of salt
- 4 cups of flour
- 2 tablespoons of baking soda
- 4 tablespoons of butter

Preparation:

Heat up your oven to about 360°. Sprinkle your yeast into your bowl of water and stir until it dissolves, add your sugar and salt and stir until it dissolves.

Add your flour and knead the mixture into a dough. Keep for 30 minutes so it can rise. Meanwhile, mix your soda with water and mix well, then cut your dough into round thick slices, dip into your soda mixture, sprinkle with salt, and bake for about 10 minutes

Rub with your oil, bake again until it becomes brownish, remove and serve.

Crab corral salad

Let's enjoy a perfect quick lunch of your favorite crab salad.

Cooking Time: 40 minutes

Yield: 4

List of Ingredients:

- 1 pound of crab meat, shredded
- 1 cup of celery, diced
- 1/2 cup of mayonnaise
- 1/3 cup of green onions, diced
- 1 tablespoon of lemon juice
- 3 boiled eggs, peeled and chopped

Preparation:

Mix your crab meat, onions, eggs, mayonnaise, celery, and lemon juice in a bowl and cover, put in your refrigerator and chill for about 40 minutes, and serve.

Conclusion

Above are 30 unique restaurant recipes that you can prepare from the comfort of your home. Hence, you don't really need to bother about visiting the restaurant with your family as it might be too expensive. Trust our recipes and enjoy!

Don't miss out!

Visit the website below and you can sign up to receive emails whenever Ida Smith publishes a new book. There's no charge and no obligation.

https://books2read.com/r/B-A-LRXL-JEFLB

BOOKS 2 READ

Connecting independent readers to independent writers.

www.ingramcontent.com/pod-product-compliance
Lightning Source LLC
Chambersburg PA
CBHW081301040426
42452CB00014B/2608

* 9 7 8 1 3 9 3 4 2 6 7 5 2 *